BUILDING MENTAL TOUGHNESS

A Practical Guide to Habit Change and Self-Control for Reaching Your Goals

BRIANNA BROOKS

Copyright © 2024 by Brianna Brooks

All rights reserved.

No part of this book may be reproduced or transmitted in any form or by any means, electronic or mechanical, including photocopying, recording, or by any information storage and retrieval system, without permission in writing from the publisher.

In a world overflowing with distractions and challenges, "Building Mental Toughness" is your essential guide to reclaiming control and achieving your goals.

Why This Book?

- **Practical, Not Preachy:** Tired of vague advice? This book offers actionable strategies, not just empty platitudes.

- **Science-Backed:** Learn how your brain works and use that knowledge to your advantage in forming lasting habits and mastering self-control.

- **Holistic Approach:** Mental toughness isn't just about willpower. This book addresses emotional regulation, supportive environments, and cultivating a growth mindset – the essential building blocks for lasting change.

- **For Everyone:** Whether you're battling procrastination, struggling with self-doubt, or simply striving to reach your full potential, this book offers the tools and guidance you need.

If you're ready to unlock the power within you and create a life of purpose, resilience, and fulfillment, this book is your roadmap.

TABLE OF CONTENTS

Introduction 7
    The Power Of Mental Toughness: Why It Matters Now More Than Ever 7
    The Science Behind Mental Resilience: A Look Into The Brain 9
    Self-Reflection Questions: 11

Chapter 1: Understanding Mental Toughness 13
    What Mental Toughness Is (And Isn't) 16
    The Four Pillars Of Mental Toughness: 19
    Self-Reflection Questions: 23
    Transformative Exercises: 24

Chapter 2: The Habit Loop - Your Brain On Autopilot 25
    How Habits Are Formed: The Neurological Pathways 27
    Identifying Your Habit Triggers: Understanding Your Cues ... 28
    Self-Reflection Questions: 32
    Transformative Exercises: 33

Chapter 3: Rewiring Your Brain - Strategies For Habit Change 34
    The Golden Rule Of Habit Change: Small Steps, Big Impact . 36
    Building New Habits: The Power Of Implementation Intentions 38
    Self-Reflection Questions: 40
    Transformative Exercises: 41

Chapter 4: Mastering Self-Control - The Art Of Emotional Regulation 43
    Understanding Emotions: The Science Of Feelings 45
    Developing Emotional Agility: Building Your Emotional Toolkit 47

Self-Reflection Questions: 49

Transformative Exercises: 50

Chapter 5: Cultivating A Growth Mindset - Embracing Challenges 52

Fixed Vs. Growth Mindset: Understanding The Difference 54

Shifting Your Perspective: Strategies For Embracing Growth 56

Self-Reflection Questions: 58

Transformative Exercises: 59

Chapter 6: Building Resilience - Bouncing Back From Setbacks 61

The Psychology Of Resilience: How To Cope With Adversity 62

Post-Traumatic Growth: Finding Strength In Difficult Times . 64

Self-Reflection Questions: 66

Transformative Exercises: 67

Chapter 7: Harnessing The Power Of Focus - Taming Your Monkey Mind 68

The Science Of Attention: Understanding Focus And Distraction 70

Mindfulness Techniques: Training Your Brain To Be Present 72

Self-Reflection Questions: 73

Transformative Exercises: 74

Chapter 8: Optimizing Your Physical Health: The Mind-Body Connection 76

The Role Of Exercise In Mental Toughness 78

Nutrition For Cognitive Function: Fueling Your Brain 79

Self-Reflection Questions: 81

Transformative Exercises: 82

Chapter 9: Creating A Supportive Environment - Building Your Tribe 83

    The Importance Of Social Support: Building Your Network... 85

    Setting Healthy Boundaries: Protecting Your Mental Energy . 87

    Self-Reflection Questions: 89

    Transformative Exercises: 90

Chapter 10: Putting It All Together - Your Personal Mental Toughness Plan 91

    Reflecting On Your Journey: Identifying Your Strengths And Weaknesses 93

    Action Steps: Creating A Personalized Plan For Ongoing Growth 95

Conclusion: Embracing A Lifetime Of Mental Toughness - Your Journey Continues 98

    Dear Reader, ... 100

INTRODUCTION

The Power of Mental Toughness: Why It Matters Now More Than Ever

Imagine trying to sip water from a firehose. That's what the modern world feels like for many of us. A relentless torrent of information bombards us daily – breaking news alerts, social media notifications, emails, texts, and endless online content. It's enough to make anyone's head spin.

But it's not just the information overload. We're also constantly comparing ourselves to the carefully curated highlight reels of others on social media, facing economic uncertainties that seem to shift with the wind, and working at a breakneck pace that leaves little time for rest or reflection.

This isn't just about a few bad days; it's a new normal. A 2022 study by the American Psychological Association revealed that stress levels are at an all-time high, with nearly 80% of adults reporting feeling stressed about the future. And it's not just our mental health that's suffering. Chronic stress has been linked to a host of physical ailments, from heart disease and stroke to diabetes and obesity.

When our mental resilience is weak, we become like ships without rudders, tossed about by the tumultuous seas of life. We succumb to burnout, anxiety, and depression. We abandon our goals at the first sign of difficulty, our dreams crumbling like sandcastles in the tide.

But imagine a different scenario for a moment. Imagine being the eye of the storm, a beacon of calm amidst the chaos. This is the power of mental toughness. It's the ability to remain grounded, focused, and motivated even when everything around you seems to fall apart.

Mental toughness is not about being emotionless or stoic. It's about acknowledging your emotions, processing them, and then choosing how you respond. It's about having the courage to face your fears and the tenacity to keep going when it gets rough.

Take, for example, the story of **Malala Yousafzai**. At just 15 years old, she was shot in the head by the Taliban for daring to speak out about girls' education. Yet, she survived and emerged stronger, becoming a Nobel Peace Prize laureate and a global advocate for girls' education. Her resilience and unwavering commitment to her cause are a shining example of mental toughness in action.

Or consider the countless entrepreneurs who have faced rejection, failure, and financial ruin yet persisted in pursuing innovation. Their unwavering belief in their vision and ability to bounce back from setbacks are hallmarks of mental toughness.

These are not just exceptional cases. Research shows that mental toughness is a key predictor of success in all areas of life, from academics and athletics to business and personal relationships. In fact, a study by the University of Pennsylvania found that mental toughness was a stronger predictor of academic success than IQ.

But how can we develop this invaluable trait? How can we transform our brains from fragile to unbreakable? The answer lies in the fascinating field of neuroscience and neuroplasticity.

The Science Behind Mental Resilience: A Look into the Brain

Your brain is not a static organ; it's more like a muscle that can be strengthened and sculpted through training. This is due to neuroplasticity, which refers to the brain's ability to change and adapt throughout life.

Think of your brain as a vast forest, with billions of neurons interconnected by intricate pathways. Every thought you have, every action you take, leaves a trace on these pathways. The more you repeat an idea or behavior, the stronger the pathway becomes, like a well-trodden path in the woods.

This is how habits are formed. But the good news is that neuroplasticity works both ways. Just as we can inadvertently create negative habits, we can also deliberately create positive ones. By consciously choosing new thoughts and behaviors and practicing them repeatedly, we can forge new neural pathways and weaken old ones. This is the essence of rewiring our brains for mental toughness.

Two key brain regions play a crucial role in this process:

- **The Prefrontal Cortex:** This is the CEO of your brain, responsible for decision-making, planning, emotional regulation, and impulse control. Strengthening this area helps you stay focused, resist temptations, and make better choices under pressure.

- **The Amygdala:** This almond-shaped structure is your brain's alarm system, triggering the fight-or-flight response when you perceive a threat. While this response is essential for survival, an overactive amygdala can lead to chronic stress and anxiety. Calming this region helps you stay cool under pressure and make rational decisions rather than reacting impulsively.

By learning to harness the power of neuroplasticity and train these key brain regions, you can literally reshape your mind for greater resilience. This is not just theoretical speculation. Scientific studies have shown that interventions like cognitive-behavioral therapy (CBT), mindfulness meditation, and even physical exercise can create positive changes in the brain, leading to improved mental toughness.

For example, research has shown that mindfulness meditation can increase the thickness of the prefrontal cortex and decrease the reactivity of the amygdala, leading to better emotional regulation and stress reduction. Similarly, studies on CBT have demonstrated its effectiveness in rewiring negative thought patterns and reducing anxicty and depression.

But mental toughness is not just about brain training. It's also about cultivating a set of core psychological skills and attitudes that enable us to navigate life's challenges with greater ease and confidence.

This book is your guide to unlocking the full potential of your mind and building unshakeable mental toughness. By understanding the science behind resilience, mastering the art of habit change, and developing a toolbox of strategies for emotional regulation and focus, you will be equipped to face any challenge that comes your way.

This is not just a self-help book; it's a roadmap to personal transformation. *It's about discovering your unbreakable spirit and unleashing your full potential. Are you ready to embark on this journey?*

Self-Reflection Questions:

1. **Personal Significance:** Why does mental toughness matter to you personally? What specific challenges in your life could benefit from increased resilience?

2. **Modern Relevance:** In what ways do you think the demands of modern life (fast pace, information overload, etc.) make mental toughness especially important today?

3. **Brain-Mind Connection:** How does understanding the brain's role in resilience change your perspective on mental toughness? Does it make it seem more achievable or less mysterious?

4. **Resilience Role Models:** Who are some people you admire for their mental toughness? What qualities do

they embody, and how might you learn from their examples?

CHAPTER 1: UNDERSTANDING MENTAL TOUGHNESS

"The difference between winning and losing is most often not quitting." – Walt Disney

Disney's words echo a profound truth: resilience, the ability to weather storms and forge ahead, often separates those who achieve their dreams from those who falter. This resilience, this unyielding spirit, is what we call mental toughness. The psychological armor shields us from the slings and arrows of outrageous fortune, the internal compass that guides us through life's labyrinthine paths.

Mental toughness isn't about brute force or stubbornness. It's not about suppressing emotions or denying the reality of hardship. Rather, it's a dynamic blend of qualities that empower us to embrace challenges, learn from setbacks, and emerge stronger on the other side. It's the unwavering belief in our ability to adapt, overcome, and ultimately thrive.

Think of mental toughness as a well-honed skillset, a finely tuned instrument we can play to create a symphony of success. Like any skill, it requires practice, dedication, and a willingness to learn from our mistakes. It's not something we're born with; it's something we build, brick by brick, through conscious effort and intentional actions.

Throughout history, mental toughness has been the driving force behind some of humanity's most remarkable achievements. **Consider the indomitable spirit of explorers like Ernest Shackleton,** who led his crew to safety after their ship was crushed in Antarctic ice. Or **the unwavering resolve of civil rights leaders like Martin Luther King Jr.,** who faced violence and oppression with unwavering courage and conviction.

In the realm of sports, we witness mental toughness every time an athlete pushes past their perceived limits, defies the odds, and achieves the seemingly impossible. **Michael Jordan, the basketball legend, famously said,** *"I've missed more than 9,000 shots in my career. I've lost almost 300 games. Twenty-six times, I've been trusted to take the game-winning shot and missed. I've failed over and over and over again in my life. And that is why I succeed."*

But mental toughness isn't just for adventurers, activists, and athletes. It's vital for success in any field, from business and entrepreneurship to education and the arts. In the fast-paced, ever-changing landscape of the modern world, mental toughness is not just an advantage; it's a necessity.

The relentless pace of technological advancement, the 24/7 news cycle, and the constant barrage of information can easily overwhelm us. The pressure to succeed, both professionally and personally, can feel suffocating. And the fear of failure, rejection, or loss can paralyze us into inaction.

But those who cultivate mental toughness can weather these storms with remarkable resilience. They don't crumble under pressure; they rise to the occasion. They don't avoid challenges; they embrace them as opportunities for growth.

They don't let setbacks define them; they learn from them and move forward with renewed determination.

The benefits of developing mental toughness are profound and far-reaching. Studies have shown that individuals with high levels of mental toughness are:

- *More likely to achieve their goals*
- *Better equipped to handle stress and adversity*
- *Less prone to anxiety and depression*
- *More satisfied with their lives*
- *More successful in their careers*
- *More resilient in the face of change*

In short, mental toughness is a superpower that can transform our lives. It empowers us to overcome obstacles, achieve our dreams, and live a life of purpose, passion, and fulfillment.

So, what does mental toughness look like in practice? It's not a single trait but a constellation of interconnected qualities that work together to create a resilient mindset. In the upcoming chapters, we will delve deeper into the core components of mental toughness, providing you with practical strategies and tools to build your unbreakable mind. We will explore the power of self-control, habit change's importance, and a growth mindset's transformative potential. But first, let's lay the foundation by understanding what mental toughness truly is – and what it isn't.

What Mental Toughness Is (and Isn't)

Mental toughness isn't about gritting teeth and plowing through adversity with a stiff upper lip. It's not about denying your emotions or pretending pain doesn't exist. These misconceptions can often do more harm than good, leading to burnout, resentment, and even physical health issues. So, what exactly is mental toughness? Let's break down the myths and unveil the truth behind this powerful concept.

What Mental Toughness Isn't:

1. **A robotic lack of emotions:** Mental toughness doesn't mean suppressing or ignoring your feelings. Instead, it involves acknowledging and processing your emotions healthily so that they don't derail you.

2. **Never asking for help:** It's not a sign of weakness to seek support when needed. Mentally tough individuals often have strong support networks and aren't afraid to ask for guidance or assistance when facing challenges.

3. **Pushing through pain at all costs:** While perseverance is important, mental toughness also involves knowing when to rest, recover, and adjust your approach. Ignoring your body's signals can lead to injury and exhaustion.

4. **Being constantly positive:** While optimism is a valuable asset, it's unrealistic to expect to be always happy. Mental toughness involves accepting negative

emotions as part of the human experience while maintaining a hopeful outlook for the future.

5. **A magical cure-all:** Mental toughness won't solve all your problems overnight. It's a skill that requires consistent practice and development over time.

What Mental Toughness Is:

1. **Resilience:** The ability to bounce back from setbacks, learn from failures, and adapt to changing circumstances. Think of a rubber band stretching under pressure but returning to its original shape. Similarly, mentally tough individuals may bend but don't break when faced with adversity.

2. **Optimism:** A positive outlook that fuels hope and perseverance. It's not about denying the existence of challenges but rather about believing in your ability to overcome them. Optimistic individuals see setbacks as temporary and focus on solutions rather than dwelling on problems.

3. **Self-belief:** The unwavering confidence in your abilities to succeed. This doesn't mean being arrogant or overestimating your skills; it means trusting your potential and believing that you have the resources within you to achieve your goals.

4. **Emotional regulation:** The capacity to manage your emotions effectively rather than letting them control you. This involves recognizing and labeling your

emotions, understanding their triggers, and developing healthy coping mechanisms to deal with stress, anxiety, and anger.

5. **Focus:** The ability to concentrate on the task at hand and resist distractions. This involves setting clear goals, prioritizing tasks, and developing strategies to maintain concentration even when faced with obstacles or setbacks.

Real-World Examples of Mental Toughness:

- **The Entrepreneur:** A startup founder faces numerous rejections from investors but maintains their belief in their product and perseveres until they secure funding.

- **The Athlete:** A marathon runner encounters a debilitating injury but returns to running through rehabilitation and a positive mindset and completes a race.

- **The Student:** A student struggles with a complex subject but seeks help from their teacher, develops effective study habits, and ultimately excels in the class.

- **The Parent:** A single parent faces financial hardship and juggles multiple responsibilities but maintains a positive attitude, focuses on providing for their children, and finds creative solutions to overcome challenges.

- **The Survivor:** A cancer patient endures grueling treatment while remaining hopeful for recovery, drawing strength from their support network and finding meaning in their experience.

The Four Pillars of Mental Toughness:

Mental toughness is not a single trait but a combination of interconnected skills and attitudes. Understanding these four pillars and actively working to develop them can significantly enhance your mental resilience and empower you to achieve your goals:

1. **COMMITMENT: THE CORNERSTONE OF SUCCESS**

   - **What it is:** The unwavering dedication to a goal or cause. It involves setting clear objectives, prioritizing actions, and staying focused despite distractions or setbacks.

   - **Why it matters:** Commitment fuels your drive and motivation, keeping you on track even when faced with obstacles or temptations. It's the engine that propels you forward and enables you to persevere through challenges.

   - **How to develop it:**
     - Set SMART goals (Specific, Measurable, Achievable, Relevant, Time-bound) that resonate with your values and aspirations.
     - Break down larger goals into smaller, more manageable steps to avoid feeling overwhelmed.

- Create a vision board or a written plan to keep your goals at the forefront of your mind.
- Identify potential obstacles and develop strategies for overcoming them.
- Surround yourself with supportive people who encourage and motivate you.

2. CONTROL: THE HELM OF YOUR SHIP

- **It is** The ability to regulate your emotions, thoughts, and behaviors. It involves managing stress, overcoming self-doubt, and maintaining composure under pressure.

- **Why it matters:** Control empowers you to respond to situations thoughtfully and deliberately rather than reacting impulsively or letting your emotions dictate your actions. It helps you stay calm and focused when facing challenges or adversity.

- **How to develop it:**
    - Practice mindfulness meditation or deep breathing exercises to increase self-awareness and emotional regulation.
    - Develop healthy coping mechanisms for managing stress and anxiety, such as exercise, spending time in nature, or talking to a trusted friend or therapist.
    - Challenge negative thoughts and replace them with more positive and empowering self-talk.

- Learn to identify and manage triggers that can lead to emotional reactivity.

3. CHALLENGE: THE CATALYST FOR GROWTH

- **What it is:** The willingness to embrace challenges as opportunities for growth. It involves viewing setbacks as learning experiences and using them to fuel personal development.

- **Why it matters:** Challenge fosters resilience and adaptability, allowing you to learn from your mistakes and emerge stronger from adversity. It encourages you to step outside your comfort zone and expand your capabilities.

- **How to develop it:**
    - Reframe challenges as opportunities for learning and growth rather than threats to your ego or self-worth.
    - Set realistic goals that stretch your abilities but are still attainable.
    - Seek out new experiences and opportunities to learn and develop new skills.
    - Celebrate your successes, but also embrace your failures as valuable lessons.
    - Surround yourself with people who challenge and inspire you to be your best.

4. CONFIDENCE: THE COMPASS OF YOUR JOURNEY

- **What it is:** The belief in your abilities to succeed. It involves a positive self-image, a can-do attitude, and the conviction that you can overcome obstacles.

- **Why it matters:** Confidence fuels your motivation, perseverance, and willingness to take risks. It helps you overcome self-doubt and believe in your ability to achieve your goals.

- **How to develop it:**

    - Identify your strengths and accomplishments, and celebrate your successes.

    - Challenge negative self-talk and replace it with positive affirmations.

    - Visualize yourself achieving your goals, and focus on the positive outcomes you desire.

    - Surround yourself with supportive people who believe in you and your potential.

    - Take on challenges that push you outside your comfort zone, and prove to yourself that you are capable of more than you think.

By understanding and embodying these four pillars, you can build unshakeable mental toughness that will empower you to navigate life's challenges with grace, resilience, and determination. Remember, mental toughness is not an innate trait but a skill that can be cultivated through deliberate practice and intentional effort. By investing in your mental resilience, you are investing in your future success and well-being.

Self-Reflection Questions:

1. **Commitment:** Think of a recent challenge you faced. How committed were you to seeing it through, even when things got tough? What factors influenced your level of commitment?

2. **Control:** Describe a situation where you felt a lack of control. What specific aspects were outside your influence? How did this lack of control affect you emotionally and behaviorally?

3. **Challenge:** Do you tend to view obstacles as roadblocks or as opportunities for growth? Give an example of a challenge you faced where you embraced it as a chance to learn and develop.

4. **Confidence:** What are your core strengths and weaknesses? How can your strengths bolster your confidence in facing challenges, and how might your weaknesses be areas for improvement?

5. **Overall Mental Toughness:** On a scale of 1 to 10, how would you rate your current level of mental toughness? What specific areas (commitment, control, challenge, confidence) do you feel strongest in, and which ones could use development?

Transformative Exercises:

1. **Commitment Visualization:** Choose a current goal. Close your eyes and vividly imagine yourself achieving it, overcoming obstacles along the way. How does this visualization make you feel? Write down a commitment statement that you can revisit regularly.

2. **Control Circle:** Draw two circles: one small, one large. In the small circle, list things you can directly control (your actions, thoughts, etc.). In the larger circle, list things you can influence but not fully control (others' reactions, certain outcomes). This helps clarify where to focus your energy.

3. **Challenge Reframing:** Think of a recent setback. Rewrite the story of this setback, focusing on the lessons learned and how it might have prepared you for future success. How does this shift your perspective?

4. **Confidence Affirmations:** Write 3-5 positive affirmations that focus on your strengths and capabilities. Repeat these daily, either out loud or in writing, to reinforce your belief in yourself.

5. **Mental Toughness Journal:** Start a journal where you track your progress in developing mental toughness. Reflect on challenges you face, how you respond, and what strategies from the four pillars you employ. Note your successes, setbacks, and lessons learned.

CHAPTER 2: THE HABIT LOOP - YOUR BRAIN ON AUTOPILOT

"We are what we repeatedly do. Excellence, then, is not an act, but a habit." – Aristotle

This ancient wisdom, penned centuries ago, rings more accurate than ever in the age of neuroscience. Our brains are wired for efficiency, constantly seeking ways to conserve energy and automate repetitive tasks. This is the essence of habit formation – the intricate dance between neurons that transforms conscious actions into automatic routines.

Consider this: approximately 40% of our daily actions are not conscious decisions but rather habits deeply ingrained in the neural pathways of our brains. These automatic behaviors, whether brushing our teeth, scrolling through social media, or biting our nails, operate beneath the surface of our awareness, silently shaping our lives.

At its core, a habit is a three-step loop consisting of a cue, a routine, and a reward. The cue is a trigger that tells your brain which habit to use, setting the wheels in motion. It could be a specific time of day, a location, an emotional state, or even the company of certain people.

The routine is the behavior – the action you take in response to the cue. This could be anything from grabbing a sugary snack when you feel stressed to lacing up your running shoes as soon as you wake up.

The reward is the payoff that reinforces the habit. It could be the pleasure of indulging in a treat, the feeling of accomplishment after a workout, or the temporary relief from stress from scrolling through your phone. This reward signals to your brain that this behavior is worth repeating, strengthening the neural connections associated with the habit loop.

Understanding this cycle is pivotal in our quest to build mental toughness. Habits are not merely mindless actions; they are the building blocks of our character, the architects of our destiny. Our habits determine our health, relationships, careers, and happiness.

Positive habits, like daily exercise, meditation, or gratitude journaling, create a virtuous growth cycle and well-being. They strengthen our mental resilience, enhance our focus, and fuel our motivation. These habits become our anchors when faced with challenges, providing stability and grounding amidst the storm.

Conversely, negative habits, such as procrastination, self-doubt, or unhealthy coping mechanisms, can erode our mental toughness. They create a vicious cycle of self-sabotage, limiting our potential and leaving us feeling stuck and unfulfilled. When we repeatedly engage in behaviors that undermine our well-being, we reinforce neural pathways that lead to negative outcomes.

But here's the empowering truth: we have the power to change our habits, to rewire our brains for greater mental toughness.

Understanding the habit loop gives us insight into the underlying mechanisms that drive our behavior. This awareness allows us to disrupt the automatic responses that no longer serve us and deliberately cultivate new, empowering habits.

One effective strategy for habit change is "habit stacking." This involves piggybacking a new habit onto an existing one, leveraging the power of established routines to create new neural pathways. For instance, if you want to develop a daily meditation practice, you could stack it onto your morning coffee ritual. After you pour your coffee, take five minutes to meditate. Over time, this new behavior will become associated with the existing habit, making it easier to stick with.

But remember, building mental toughness through habit change is not a quick fix or a magic bullet. It requires patience, persistence, and a willingness to experiment and adapt.

How Habits Are Formed: The Neurological Pathways

Think of your brain as a vast network of roads and highways, with billions of neurons acting as bustling intersections. Every time you act, you send a signal along a particular route in this network. The more you repeat the action, the more worn in that path becomes, making it easier and faster for signals to travel along it in the future. This is the essence of habit formation – the creation of well-trodden neural pathways that enable automatic behavior.

The neurotransmitter dopamine, often called the "feel-good" chemical, is at the heart of this process. When you engage in a pleasurable activity – eating a delicious meal, receiving a compliment, or achieving a goal – your brain releases dopamine, creating a sense of reward and satisfaction. This reward signal reinforces the behavior, making you more likely to repeat it in the future.

The basal ganglia, a cluster of structures deep within the brain, play a crucial role in this reward-based learning. They act like a switchboard, connecting the cue that triggers a habit (e.g., seeing a notification on your phone) to the routine behavior (e.g., checking your social media feed) and the resulting reward (e.g., the dopamine hit from seeing a like or comment). This process is known as the habit loop.

Over time, as you repeatedly engage in a behavior, the connection between the cue and the routine becomes stronger, and the behavior becomes increasingly automatic. It requires less and less conscious effort until it eventually becomes a habit.

Identifying Your Habit Triggers: Understanding Your Cues

Breaking free from the grip of unwanted habits and cultivating new, empowering ones requires a deep understanding of your habit triggers. These cues can be external, such as specific locations, times of day, or social situations, or internal, such as emotions, thoughts, or bodily sensations.

To identify your habit triggers, start by paying close attention to your daily routines. When do you engage in the habit? Where are you? Who are you with? What are you feeling or thinking? By observing your patterns, you can begin to pinpoint the cues that initiate the automatic response.

Here are some helpful journaling prompts and self-reflection exercises to uncover your triggers:

- **Habit Tracker:** For a week or two, keep a daily log of your habits. Note the time, location, and thoughts or feelings preceding the habit. This will help you identify patterns and correlations.

- **The "Why" Behind the Habit:** Ask yourself why you engage in the habit. What need is it fulfilling? Are you seeking pleasure, avoiding discomfort, or responding to a particular emotion?

- **Scenario Analysis:** Imagine yourself in different situations and consider how you might react. Would you be more or less likely to engage in the habit under other circumstances?

Once you've identified your triggers, you can develop strategies for managing them. This might involve avoiding specific environments, changing your routine, or finding alternative ways to satisfy the underlying need that the habit was fulfilling.

Interrupting the Automatic Response: Creating Space for Conscious Choice

Breaking a habit isn't just about willpower; it's about creating a pause between the trigger and the routine, a space for conscious choice. This interruption lets you recognize your habitual response and choose a different action.

Here are some practical strategies for interrupting the automatic response:

- **Mindfulness:** When you notice a habit trigger, pause and take a few deep breaths. Observe your thoughts and feelings without judgment. This simple act of awareness can create enough space to make a conscious decision.

- **Substitution:** Replace the unwanted habit with a more desirable behavior that fulfills the same need. For example, if you tend to reach for sugary snacks when you're stressed, try going for a walk or talking to a friend instead.

- **Rewards:** Reward yourself for successfully resisting the habit. This positive reinforcement can help strengthen the new neural pathways you're creating.

- **Environmental Design:** Modify your environment to make the unwanted habit more difficult and the desired behavior easier. For example, if you want to reduce screen time, put your phone in another room or delete distracting apps.

Habit Audit: Your Personal Roadmap to Change

To gain a deeper understanding of your habit patterns and identify areas for improvement, it can be helpful to conduct a "habit audit." This involves systematically reviewing your daily routines and identifying both the habits that serve you well and those that are holding you back.

Here's how to get started:

1. **List Your Habits:** Write down all of the habits you engage in on a daily basis, both positive and negative.
2. **Categorize Your Habits:** Group your habits into categories, such as health, productivity, relationships, or personal growth.
3. **Evaluate Your Habits:** Rate each habit on a scale of 1 to 5, with 1 being "very unhelpful" and 5 being "very helpful."
4. **Identify Areas for Improvement:** Focus on the habits that you rated as unhelpful or neutral. These are the areas where you can make the most significant changes.
5. **Create an Action Plan:** Develop a plan for modifying or replacing these unwanted habits with more empowering ones.

Remember, building mental toughness is a journey, not a destination. Rewiring your brain and establishing new habits takes time, effort, and commitment. But by understanding the science behind habit formation and applying the strategies outlined in this chapter, you can unlock your full potential and achieve your goals.

The journey to mental toughness starts with understanding your habits. By harnessing the power of your brain, you can break free from the autopilot mode and create a life that is truly your own.

Self-Reflection Questions:

1. **Habit Awareness:** What are 3-5 habits you currently have that you'd like to change? For each one, try to identify the routine (the behavior itself), the reward (what you get out of it), and the trigger (what cues the habit).

2. **Trigger Analysis:** Think of a specific habit you're trying to change. When and where does this habit usually occur? What are its most common triggers (specific locations, emotions, people, times of day)?

3. **Reward System:** What reward does it provide you for a challenging habit you're trying to break? Is it a physical sensation, an emotional release, a distraction? Understanding this reward can help you find healthier substitutes.

4. **Habit Strength:** On a scale of 1-10, how ingrained do you feel each of your identified habits is? Which ones feel most automatic and resistant to change?

5. **Neurological Awareness:** How does understanding the neurological basis of habits (the habit loop) change your perception of your own behaviors? Does it make you feel more empowered to create change?

Transformative Exercises:

1. **Habit Tracker:** Create a chart or use a habit-tracking app to monitor your chosen habits for a week. Note whether you engage in the habit or successfully resist it each time the trigger occurs. This can reveal patterns and help you identify alternative responses.

2. **Trigger Modification:** Choose one habit trigger to modify. If it's a location (e.g., snacking in front of the TV), change the environment. If it's an emotional trigger (e.g., mindfulness, exercise), develop healthier coping mechanisms.

3. **Reward Substitution:** For a habit with an unhealthy reward, brainstorm alternative activities that provide a similar type of satisfaction. Experiment with these substitutes to see what works best.

4. **Habit Disruption:** Intentionally disrupt a habit's routine. If you always brush your teeth with your right hand, try using your left. This forces you to be more mindful and can weaken the automatic nature of the habit.

5. **Mindful Habit Creation:** Choose a positive habit you'd like to cultivate. Design a clear routine for it, identify a specific trigger, and choose a rewarding consequence. Practice this new habit loop consistently, using mindfulness to reinforce it.

CHAPTER 3: REWIRING YOUR BRAIN - STRATEGIES FOR HABIT CHANGE

Your brain is not set in stone. Contrary to the adage that **you can't teach an old dog new tricks, your brain is a dynamic, ever-evolving organ capable of remarkable transformation.** This inherent flexibility, known as neuroplasticity, is the key to unlocking the potential for profound change in your life.

Imagine your brain as a bustling city with intricate networks of roads representing neural pathways. Each thought, action, and experience carve out these pathways, making it easier for signals to travel along familiar routes. Habits, whether beneficial or detrimental, are formed through this process of repeated neural activation. The more you engage in a particular behavior, the deeper and more ingrained these pathways become.

But here's the exciting part: just as new roads can be built and old ones rerouted in a city, your brain can create new neural connections and modify existing ones. This is the essence of neuroplasticity, the brain's ability to reorganize itself in response to new experiences and learning.

This extraordinary phenomenon is not confined to childhood or adolescence; it persists throughout our lives. Even as adults, we can rewire our brains, transforming our habits, thoughts, and behaviors. This means that even the most ingrained habits are not immutable. With the right tools and strategies, you can break free from unwanted patterns and cultivate positive ones.

So, how do we harness the power of neuroplasticity to create lasting change? The answer lies in a multi-faceted approach that combines various evidence-based strategies, each targeting different aspects of the habit change process.

Mindfulness, the practice of paying non-judgmental attention to the present moment, can be a powerful tool for habit change. By becoming more aware of our thoughts, feelings, and bodily sensations, we can gain valuable insights into the triggers that drive our habits. With this awareness, we can make conscious choices about how to respond to these triggers, rather than reacting on autopilot.

Visualization techniques, which involve mentally rehearsing desired behaviors, can also be effective in creating new neural pathways. By vividly imagining ourselves performing the desired action, we activate the same brain regions as if we were doing it, priming our neural circuits for change.

Cognitive reframing, challenging and changing negative thought patterns, can help us overcome the mental roadblocks that often sabotage our efforts to change. By replacing self-defeating thoughts with empowering ones, we can reprogram our minds for success.

Environmental design involves strategically modifying our surroundings to make adopting new habits easier and breaking old ones. We can create an environment that supports our goals by removing tempting cues for unwanted behaviors and creating visual reminders for desired actions.

These are just a few evidence-based strategies for leveraging neuroplasticity and rewiring your brain for positive change. By experimenting with different techniques and finding what works best for you, you can create a personalized toolkit for habit transformation.

However, it's important to remember that habit change takes time and effort. It takes time, effort, and commitment. There will be setbacks along the way, but it's crucial to approach these with self-compassion and understanding. Instead of viewing setbacks as failures, see them as valuable learning experiences that can help you refine your approach and strengthen your resolve.

The Golden Rule of Habit Change: Small Steps, Big Impact

Embarking on a journey to transform your habits might seem like a daunting task, an uphill battle against deeply ingrained routines. But what if the secret to lasting change lies not in grand, sweeping gestures, but in the subtle power of small steps?

Imagine trying to climb Mount Everest in a single leap. It's impossible, right? You'd exhaust yourself before even making a dent. The same principle applies to habit change. Drastic overhauls rarely work in the long run because they overwhelm our willpower and often lead to burnout. Our brains are wired to resist sudden, dramatic changes.

Instead, the most sustainable and effective path to habit change is paved with small, incremental adjustments. This approach aligns with the way our brains naturally learn and adapt. Each time you perform a new behavior, even a small one, you strengthen the neural connections associated with it. Over time, these connections become stronger and more efficient, making it easier to repeat the behavior automatically.

Think of it like building a muscle. You wouldn't expect to bench-press 200 pounds on your first day at the gym. Instead, you start with a weight you can manage and gradually increase it over time. Similarly, when changing habits, it's crucial to start with manageable steps and gradually increase the difficulty as you build strength and confidence.

This "small steps" approach is not only more sustainable, but it's also more effective in the long run. Research has shown that individuals who make small, consistent changes are more likely to stick with their new habits and achieve their goals than those who attempt radical transformations.

Consider the story of a woman named Angela who wanted to improve her fitness. Instead of jumping into a rigorous exercise program, she started by walking for just 15 minutes each day. After a few weeks, she increased her walking time to 20 minutes, then 30 minutes, and so on. Eventually, she felt confident enough to incorporate other forms of exercise, like jogging and strength training. Within a year, she had completely transformed her lifestyle and achieved a level of fitness she had never thought possible.

Another example is the story of a man named David who wanted to overcome his procrastination habit. Instead of trying to tackle all his tasks at once, he started by committing to completing just one small task each day. This could be as simple as replying to an email, making a phone call, or cleaning out a drawer. Over time, he gradually increased the number of tasks he completed each day, and within a few months, he had significantly improved his productivity and reduced his stress levels.

These stories illustrate the power of small steps. By breaking down large goals into smaller, more manageable actions, we make them seem less daunting and more achievable. Each small victory builds momentum and reinforces the desired behavior, making it easier to stick with it over time.

If the prospect of change feels overwhelming, remember that you don't have to do it all at once. Start small. Choose one habit you want to change and break it down into tiny, manageable steps. Focus on making one small improvement each day, and over time, these small steps will add up to significant change.

Be patient with yourself. Habit change is a process, not an event. There will be setbacks and challenges along the way, but don't let them discourage you. View them as learning opportunities and adjust your approach accordingly.

Building New Habits: The Power of Implementation Intentions

One powerful tool for building new habits is the implementation intention. This is a simple yet effective strategy that involves creating a specific plan for when and where you will perform a desired behavior. The format is simple: "If situation X arises, then I will perform response Y."

For example, if you want to start exercising regularly, your implementation intention might be: "If it's 7 AM on Monday, Wednesday, and Friday, then I will go for a 30-minute walk." This pre-determined plan eliminates the need for decision-making in the moment, making it more likely that you will follow through with your desired action.

Implementation intentions work because they leverage the brain's natural tendency to follow through on commitments. By creating a specific plan, you are essentially pre-programming your brain to respond automatically to certain cues. This reduces the mental energy required to make decisions and increases the likelihood of taking action.

Numerous studies have shown the effectiveness of implementation intentions in promoting habit change. In one study, participants who created implementation intentions for exercising were significantly more likely to stick with their exercise routine than those who simply set goals without specific plans.

Here's how you can create effective implementation intentions:

1. **Identify the habit you want to build:** Be specific and clear about what you want to achieve. Instead of saying, "I want to eat healthier," say, "I want to eat a salad for lunch every day."

2. **Choose a specific time and place:** When and where will you perform the desired behavior? This could be as simple as, "After I brush my teeth in the morning, I will meditate for 5 minutes."

3. **Write down your implementation intention:** Putting it in writing helps solidify your commitment and makes it easier to remember. You can even post it somewhere visible as a reminder.

4. **Track your progress:** Monitor how often you follow through with your implementation intention. This will help you identify any obstacles or challenges that need to be addressed.

5. **Adjust your plan as needed:** If you find that your implementation intention isn't working, don't be afraid to modify it. Experiment with different times, places, or behaviors until you find something that works for you.

The power of implementation intentions lies in their simplicity and effectiveness. By creating specific plans for when and where you will perform desired behaviors, you can significantly increase your chances of success in building new habits and achieving your goals.

Self-Reflection Questions:

1. **Small Wins:** What small, manageable changes could you make to your target habit that might lead to a big impact over time? How can you break down your larger goal into smaller, achievable steps?

2. **Current Approach:** Reflect on your past attempts to change habits. Did you try to change too much too soon? Were your goals unrealistic, or do you need to be more specific? How can you apply the "small steps" principle to your current efforts?

3. **Implementation Intentions:** Have you ever used implementation intentions before? If so, how effective were they? What specific "if-then" statements could you create to support your habit change goals if not?

4. **Habit Stacking:** Are there any existing habits you could "stack" a new habit onto? For example, if you want to meditate daily, could you do it right after brushing your teeth in the morning?

5. **Motivation and Obstacles:** What motivates you most to change this particular habit? What obstacles do you anticipate, and how can you prepare to overcome them using the strategies in this chapter?

Transformative Exercises:

1. **Habit Change Plan:** Create a detailed plan for changing your target habit, breaking it down into small, measurable steps. Use the "golden rule" to guide your approach, focusing on gradual progress.

2. **Implementation Intention Practice:** Write 3-5 "if-then" statements about your habit change goal. For example, "If it's 7 AM, then I will meditate for 10

minutes." Practice using these statements daily to reinforce the desired behavior.

3. **Habit Stacking Experiment:** Choose an existing habit as a trigger for a new habit you want to develop. For one week, practice linking the two behaviors consistently. Reflect on how this strategy affects your success.

4. **Tiny Habits Challenge:** Commit to practicing a "tiny habit" related to your goal for one week. This could be as simple as doing one push-up every time you leave your bedroom. Notice how this small action builds momentum and motivation.

5. **Visual Reminders:** Create visual cues to help you remember your implementation intentions and habit goals. These could be sticky notes, phone reminders, or images representing your desired behavior.

CHAPTER 4: MASTERING SELF-CONTROL - THE ART OF EMOTIONAL REGULATION

"The first and best victory is to conquer self." Plato's timeless wisdom echoes through the ages, highlighting a truth that remains as relevant today as it was in ancient Greece: self-control is the cornerstone of personal mastery. But what exactly is self-control, and how does it relate to the complex interplay of emotions, thoughts, and behaviors?

Self-control is the ability to manage our impulses, emotions, and desires in pursuit of our goals. It's the inner strength that allows us to resist temptation, delay gratification, and make choices aligned with our values, even when faced with immediate gratification.

This intricate dance between our inner world and outer actions is a symphony of interconnected processes. Emotions, often triggered by external events or internal thoughts, are rapid, automatic responses that prepare us to act. Thoughts, on the other hand, are the interpretations we give to these emotions, shaping our understanding of the situation and influencing our subsequent behavior.

Imagine this scenario: you're stuck in traffic on your way to an important meeting. Your initial emotion might be frustration or anger, triggered by the inconvenience and potential consequences of being late. Your thoughts might race, dwelling on the unfairness of the situation or the incompetence of other drivers. These thoughts, in turn, can intensify your emotions, leading to a surge of adrenaline and a desire to lash out, honk your horn, or make risky maneuvers.

However, if you possess strong self-control, you're able to pause, take a deep breath, and challenge those thoughts. You might remind yourself that anger won't solve the problem or that you can still make the most of the situation by catching up on emails or listening to a podcast. By reframing your thoughts, you can de-escalate your emotions and choose a more constructive course of action, such as calmly notifying your colleagues of the delay and using the extra time to mentally prepare for the meeting.

This example highlights the crucial role of self-control in navigating the complex relationship between emotions, thoughts, and behaviors. When we lack self-control, we become puppets to our impulses, reacting instinctively to whatever emotions or thoughts arise. This can lead to regrettable actions, strained relationships, and missed opportunities.

Conversely, when we cultivate self-control, we gain the ability to choose our responses rather than being controlled by them. We can acknowledge our emotions without being overwhelmed by them, challenge our thoughts to ensure they are accurate and helpful, and make decisions that align with our long-term goals and values.

But self-control is not simply about suppressing our emotions or desires. It's about understanding them, harnessing their energy, and channeling them in productive directions. For instance, if you're feeling anxious about an upcoming presentation, instead of trying to ignore or deny your anxiety, you can use it as a motivator to prepare thoroughly and practice your delivery.

Self-control is also not about being perfect. We all have moments of weakness and impulsivity. The key is to learn from these experiences, forgive ourselves, and move forward with renewed determination. It's about recognizing that self-control is a skill that can be developed through practice and perseverance.

Research has shown that self-control is like a muscle that can be strengthened over time. Just as lifting weights repeatedly builds physical strength, engaging in activities that require self-control can enhance our ability to regulate our emotions, resist temptations, and make better choices. This can involve simple exercises like delaying gratification, resisting urges, or practicing mindfulness.

The benefits of developing self-control are manifold. Studies have linked it to improved academic performance, healthier relationships, greater financial stability, and even increased longevity. In essence, self-control empowers us to create the lives we want, rather than being at the mercy of our impulses and emotions.

Understanding Emotions: The Science of Feelings

Emotions are an integral part of the human experience, coloring our lives with vibrant hues of joy, sorrow, anger, fear, and everything in between. They are the subtle whispers and the resounding roars that guide our actions, shape our thoughts, and influence our relationships. But what exactly are emotions? How do they arise within us, and what roles do they play in our lives?

At their core, emotions are complex psychophysiological experiences that involve a symphony of bodily sensations, thoughts, and behavioral urges. When we encounter a stimulus, whether it's a heartwarming hug or a looming deadline, our brains swiftly interpret its significance and trigger a cascade of physiological changes. Our heart rate may quicken, our muscles may tense, our palms may sweat – these are the telltale signs of our bodies preparing to respond to the perceived threat or reward.

But emotions are not merely physical sensations. They also encompass a rich tapestry of thoughts and interpretations. Our brains analyze the situation, drawing upon our past experiences, cultural norms, and personal beliefs to make sense of the event and determine its emotional relevance. These interpretations, in turn, give rise to specific feelings like joy, anger, or fear, which then motivate us to act in certain ways.

The intricate interplay between bodily sensations, thoughts, and behavioral urges is beautifully encapsulated in the concept of "emotional granularity." This term refers to the ability to label emotions with specificity and nuance, rather than relying on broad, generic terms like "good" or "bad." Research has shown that individuals with high emotional granularity possess greater insight into their own feelings, are better equipped to regulate their emotions, and enjoy stronger mental well-being.

Developing Emotional Agility: Building Your Emotional Toolkit

Imagine a skilled carpenter with a toolbox overflowing with various tools, each carefully selected for specific tasks. Just as a carpenter relies on their tools to craft intricate masterpieces, we can equip ourselves with an "emotional toolkit" to navigate the complex landscape of our feelings. This toolkit is built upon the foundation of emotional intelligence, a multifaceted concept that encompasses the ability to recognize, understand, and manage our own emotions as well as the emotions of others.

One of the most powerful tools in our emotional toolkit is mindfulness. This practice involves paying non-judgmental attention to our present-moment experiences, including our thoughts, feelings, and bodily sensations. By cultivating mindfulness, we can develop a heightened awareness of our emotions as they arise, allowing us to respond to them with greater clarity and intention.

Another valuable tool is cognitive reappraisal. This involves consciously reframing our interpretations of events, shifting our perspectives to create more adaptive emotional responses. For example, instead of viewing a challenging situation as a threat, we might reframe it as an opportunity for growth and learning.

Stress management tools, such as deep breathing exercises, progressive muscle relaxation, and guided imagery, can also play a vital role in our emotional toolkit. These techniques help us to calm our minds and bodies, reducing the physiological arousal that often accompanies intense emotions.

In addition to these tools, it's important to cultivate healthy coping mechanisms for dealing with challenging emotions like anger, anxiety, and sadness. This might involve engaging in activities that bring us joy, seeking support from loved ones, or seeking professional help if needed. Remember, there's no shame in asking for help – it's a sign of strength and self-awareness.

Developing emotional agility is not only beneficial for our personal well-being, but it also has a profound impact on our relationships, communication, and conflict resolution skills. By understanding and managing our emotions effectively, we can build stronger connections with others, express ourselves more authentically, and navigate disagreements with grace and understanding.

Incorporating Emotional Agility into Your Mental Toughness Journey

In the pursuit of building mental toughness, emotional agility serves as a vital pillar. By mastering the art of recognizing, understanding, and managing our emotions, we become better equipped to handle challenges, setbacks, and adversity with resilience and grace.

- **Habit Change and Self-Control:** Emotional agility empowers us to break free from unhealthy patterns and develop positive habits. When we understand the emotional triggers that drive our behaviors, we can make conscious choices that align with our goals and values.

- **Reaching Your Goals:** By harnessing the power of our emotions, we can tap into a wellspring of motivation and perseverance. Emotions like enthusiasm, passion, and determination can fuel our efforts and propel us towards our desired outcomes.

The journey towards mental toughness is not about suppressing or denying our emotions. It's about embracing them as valuable sources of information, learning from them, and using them to our advantage. By cultivating emotional agility, we can transform our emotions from potential obstacles into powerful allies in our quest for personal growth and success.

Self-Reflection Questions:

1. **Emotional Awareness:** How aware are you of your emotions as they arise? Can you identify specific bodily sensations, thoughts, or behaviours that signal different emotions?

2. **Emotional Vocabulary:** How extensive is your vocabulary for describing emotions? Do you tend to use broad terms (happy, sad, angry), or can you articulate more nuanced feelings (frustrated, disappointed, anxious)?

3. **Emotional Triggers:** What are your common emotional triggers? Are certain situations, people, or thoughts reliably evoke specific emotions in you?

4. **Emotional Coping Mechanisms:** How do you typically cope with intense emotions? Are your coping mechanisms healthy and constructive, or do they tend to be avoidant or destructive?

5. **Emotional Agility:** How adaptable are you when experiencing difficult emotions? Can you acknowledge them without judgment, explore them with curiosity, and move through them with resilience?

Transformative Exercises:

1. **Emotion Labeling:** Practice labelling your emotions as you experience them throughout the day. Use specific, descriptive language to identify the nuances of your feelings. This can increase your emotional awareness and understanding.

2. **Emotion Wheel:** Explore an emotion wheel (available online) to expand your emotional vocabulary. Identify emotions you might not be familiar with, and try to relate them to your own experiences.

3. **Trigger Tracker:** Keep a journal to track your emotional triggers for a week. Note the situation, thoughts, bodily sensations, and the emotions that arise. Look for patterns that can help you anticipate and manage triggers more effectively.

4. **Mindful Breathing:** Practice mindful breathing exercises when you feel overwhelmed by emotions. Focus on the sensation of your breath entering and

leaving your body, allowing thoughts and feelings to come and go without judgment.

5. **Emotional Agility Practice:** When you experience a complex emotion, try the "RAIN" technique:

    - **R**ecognize: Acknowledge the emotion without judgment.
    - **A**llow: Allow yourself to feel the emotion without resistance.
    - **I**nvestigate: Explore the emotion with curiosity, noticing its sensations and effects.
    - **N**urture: Offer yourself self-compassion and support as you move through the emotion.

Remember, developing emotional agility is an ongoing process. Be patient with yourself, and celebrate your progress as you learn to navigate the complexities of your emotional landscape.

CHAPTER 5: CULTIVATING A GROWTH MINDSET - EMBRACING CHALLENGES

"The difference between ordinary and extraordinary is that little extra." - Jimmy Johnson

This quote perfectly encapsulates the essence of a growth mindset—the belief that our abilities are not fixed but can be developed through dedication and hard work. It's the "little extra" that separates those who thrive in the face of challenges from those who shrink away.

Imagine two individuals faced with the same daunting task. One, with a fixed mindset believes their intelligence and talents are set in stone. They avoid challenges, fear failure, and see effort as a sign of inadequacy. The other, embracing a growth mindset, views challenges as opportunities to learn and expand their abilities. They see effort as a path to mastery and welcome feedback as a chance to improve.

The contrast is stark. The individual with a fixed mindset will likely become discouraged, give up easily, and stagnate. On the other hand, a person with a growth mindset will persevere, learn from their mistakes, and continue to grow and evolve.

This fundamental difference in mindset has a profound impact on our lives. It affects how we approach learning, handle setbacks, and ultimately, how much we achieve. Research has shown that individuals with a growth mindset are more resilient, creative, motivated, and satisfied with their lives.

Why is this? A growth mindset creates a love of learning rather than a hunger for approval. It allows us to embrace challenges and setbacks as opportunities for growth rather than threats to our self-worth. It encourages us to persevere in the face of obstacles, knowing that our efforts will eventually lead to improvement.

In essence, a growth mindset not only empowers us to reach our full potential, but it also transforms obstacles into stepping stones and setbacks into springboards. It shifts our focus from proving ourselves to improving ourselves. And in a world that is constantly changing and evolving, this ability to adapt and grow is more important than ever.

Adopting a growth mindset is not about becoming an overnight success or magically acquiring new talents. It's about changing the way we think about our abilities and embracing the process of learning and growth. It's about seeing challenges as opportunities, effort as a path to mastery, and setbacks as valuable lessons. It's about believing in our potential to change and evolve.

The great news is that a growth mindset can be cultivated. It requires a conscious effort to shift our beliefs and attitudes, but it's a shift that can have a transformative impact on our lives. By embracing challenges, valuing effort, learning from mistakes, and seeking feedback, we can unlock our full potential and achieve our goals.

In the next sections, we will delve deeper into the science behind mindsets, explore practical and actionable strategies for cultivating a growth mindset, and discuss how to apply this mindset to different areas of our lives. Whether you're striving to improve your career, your relationships, or your personal well-being, a growth mindset can provide the foundation for lasting success and fulfillment.

Fixed vs. Growth Mindset: Understanding the Difference

Our mindset, the lens through which we view our abilities and potential, plays a pivotal role in shaping our lives. At the heart of this concept lies the distinction between a fixed mindset and a growth mindset. Understanding this difference is crucial for building mental toughness and achieving our goals.

Individuals with a **fixed mindset** believe that their intelligence, talents, and abilities are fixed traits. They see these qualities as innate and unchanging, leading to a fear of failure and a tendency to avoid challenges. This fear stems from the belief that if they don't succeed, it reflects a fundamental flaw in their capabilities. As a result, they may shy away from situations that could expose their perceived weaknesses, preferring to stick to what they know they can do well.

In contrast, those with a **growth mindset** view intelligence, talents, and abilities as malleable qualities that can be developed through effort and learning. They embrace challenges as opportunities for growth, recognizing that setbacks are not failures but valuable learning experiences. This mindset fosters a love of learning, a willingness to take risks, and a belief in continuous improvement. People with a growth mindset are not afraid to step outside their comfort zones, as they understand that even if they don't succeed initially, they can learn from their mistakes and come back stronger.

Real-World Examples: Contrasting Mindsets in Action

To better grasp the impact of these mindsets, consider these real-world examples:

1. **The Student Facing a Difficult Exam:**
    - **Fixed Mindset:** A student with a fixed mindset might panic, convinced that they are not smart enough to pass. They may resort to cramming or even cheating, hoping to scrape by without exposing their perceived lack of ability.
    - **Growth Mindset:** A student with a growth mindset would view the exam as a challenge to overcome. They would study diligently, seeking help from their teacher or peers if needed, and focus on mastering the material rather than just passing the test.

2. **The Athlete Overcoming an Injury:**
    - **Fixed Mindset:** An athlete with a fixed mindset might see their injury as a sign that they are no longer capable of competing at a high level. They may give up on their sport altogether, feeling defeated and discouraged.

- **Growth Mindset:** An athlete with a growth mindset would see their injury as a temporary setback. They would focus on rehabilitation and recovery, determined to come back stronger than ever.

Shifting Your Perspective: Strategies for Embracing Growth

The good news is that mindsets are not set in stone. It is possible to shift from a fixed mindset to a growth mindset, unlocking a world of possibilities for personal and professional development. Here are some actionable strategies:

1. **Reframe Challenges as Opportunities:** Instead of viewing challenges as threats, see them as opportunities to learn and grow. Embrace the discomfort of stepping outside your comfort zone, knowing that it is through these experiences that you will expand your skills and knowledge.

2. **Celebrate Effort over Innate Talent:** Shift your focus from praising innate talent to celebrating effort, perseverance, and resilience. Recognize that even the most gifted individuals need to put in hard work to achieve their goals.

3. **Focus on Progress, Not Perfection:** Let go of the need to be perfect and embrace the journey of continuous improvement. Set realistic goals, track your progress, and celebrate small victories along the way.

4. **Practice Positive Self-Talk:** Replace negative self-talk with positive affirmations. Remind yourself that you are capable of learning and growing, and that setbacks are simply stepping stones on the path to success.

5. **Surround Yourself with Growth-Minded Individuals:** Seek out mentors, friends, and colleagues who embody a growth mindset. Their positive attitudes and encouragement can be infectious and inspire you to adopt a similar perspective.

Personal Anecdotes and Case Studies:

Countless individuals have experienced transformative changes in their lives by adopting a growth mindset. From students who overcame academic challenges to entrepreneurs who built successful businesses despite initial failures, the power of a growth mindset is undeniable.

One inspiring example is Carol Dweck, the psychologist who pioneered the concept of mindset. In her book *Mindset: The New Psychology of Success,* she shares numerous stories of people who have transformed their lives by embracing a growth mindset. For instance, she tells the story of a student who struggled with math but went on to become a successful engineer after realizing that he could improve his abilities through hard work and dedication.

Cultivating a Growth Mindset for Building Mental Toughness

Incorporating a growth mindset into your mental toughness journey can be a game-changer.

- **Habit Change and Self-Control:** When faced with the challenge of changing a habit, a growth mindset encourages you to view it as a learning process rather than a test of willpower. You're more likely to persevere, knowing that setbacks are not failures but opportunities to refine your approach.

- **Reaching Your Goals:** A growth mindset fuels your motivation to strive for ambitious goals. You see obstacles not as insurmountable barriers but as challenges to be conquered. This resilience in the face of adversity is a hallmark of mental toughness.

Self-Reflection Questions:

1. **Mindset Identification:** When faced with a challenge, do you tend to think, "I'm not good at this" (fixed) or "I can learn how to do this" (growth)? What are some common phrases you use that might reveal your underlying mindset?

2. **Past Experiences:** Recall a time when you succeeded at something you initially found difficult. Did you attribute your success to innate talent or to effort and perseverance? How did this belief affect your motivation and future actions?

3. **Fear of Failure:** How does the fear of failure influence your decisions and actions? Does it hold you back from taking risks or trying new things?

4. **Feedback Response:** When you receive constructive criticism or feedback, do you see it as a personal attack or as an opportunity to learn and improve?

5. **Growth Areas:** In what areas of your life would you like to adopt a more growth-oriented mindset? Are there specific skills you want to develop or challenges you want to overcome?

Transformative Exercises:

1. **Challenge Reframing:** Choose a current challenge you're facing. Instead of viewing it as a threat or an obstacle, reframe it as an opportunity to learn and grow. Ask yourself: "What can I gain from this experience?"

2. **Failure Reframing:** Think of a past failure or setback. Instead of dwelling on the negative aspects, identify the lessons you learned and how they have helped you grow. Write a new narrative for this experience, focusing on its positive impact.

3. **Growth Mindset Affirmations:** Write down several affirmations that resonate with a growth mindset, such as "I embrace challenges as opportunities to learn" or "My effort and dedication determine my success." Repeat these affirmations daily to reinforce your belief in your ability to grow.

4. **Role Model Inspiration:** Identify individuals you admire for their growth mindset. Study their stories and learn from their strategies for overcoming challenges and achieving success.

CHAPTER 6: BUILDING RESILIENCE - BOUNCING BACK FROM SETBACKS

"Our greatest glory is not in never falling, but in rising every time we fall." - Confucius

Resilience isn't about avoiding life's storms, it's about learning to dance in the rain. It's the cornerstone of mental toughness, the inner strength that empowers us to overcome adversity, bounce back from setbacks, and continue moving forward.

Resilience is not an innate trait; it's a dynamic process that can be cultivated and strengthened over time. It involves a complex interplay of individual characteristics, environmental factors, and learned coping mechanisms. Think of it as a multi-faceted gem, with each facet contributing to its overall brilliance.

At the heart of resilience lie individual characteristics such as optimism, adaptability, and problem-solving skills. Optimists tend to view challenges as temporary and surmountable, focusing on solutions rather than dwelling on problems. Adaptable individuals are flexible and open to change, able to adjust their strategies when faced with new circumstances. Strong problem-solving skills enable individuals to break down complex challenges into manageable steps, finding creative solutions to overcome obstacles.

Beyond individual traits, environmental factors play a crucial role in fostering resilience. Strong social support networks provide a safety net, offering encouragement, guidance, and practical assistance during difficult times. Access to resources, such as education, healthcare, and financial stability, can also enhance resilience by providing individuals with the tools and opportunities they need to thrive.

While some individuals may seem naturally more resilient than others, it's important to remember that resilience is not a fixed trait. It's a skill that can be learned and honed through practice and experience. Just as a muscle grows stronger with exercise, our resilience can be strengthened by facing challenges head-on and learning from our setbacks.

The Psychology of Resilience: How to Cope with Adversity

Life is a tapestry woven with threads of joy, sorrow, triumph, and adversity. While we cannot always control the events that unfold, we can cultivate the inner strength to navigate life's challenges with resilience. Resilience is not about avoiding pain or hardship; it's about adapting and returning from adversity with renewed vigor and wisdom. Understanding the psychological mechanisms that underpin resilience can empower us to develop this invaluable life skill.

Self-Efficacy:

Self-efficacy, the belief in one's ability to succeed in specific situations, is a cornerstone of resilience. When faced with adversity, individuals with high self-efficacy are more likely to view challenges as opportunities for growth rather than insurmountable obstacles. They approach difficulties with a can-do attitude, believing that they have the skills and resources to overcome them. This belief fuels their motivation and perseverance, enabling them to bounce back from setbacks with renewed determination.

Self-Compassion:

Self-compassion involves treating oneself with kindness and understanding, especially during struggle. It is the antidote to self-criticism and negative self-talk, which can erode resilience. When we practice self-compassion, we acknowledge our pain and suffering without judgment, recognizing that everyone experiences setbacks and failures. This self-acceptance allows us to move forward with greater emotional stability and resilience.

Sense of Purpose:

A sense of purpose, a belief in something larger than oneself, provides a powerful source of resilience. When we have a clear purpose in life, we are more likely to find meaning in our experiences, even the difficult ones. This meaning can serve as a guiding light during times of adversity, helping us to maintain hope and persevere through challenges. A sense of purpose can be found in various aspects of life, such as career, family, community, or spirituality.

Practical Strategies for Building Resilience:

1. **Develop Healthy Coping Mechanisms:** Identify healthy ways to manage stress and difficult emotions. This could involve exercise, meditation, journaling, spending time in nature, or engaging in creative activities.

2. **Cultivate Gratitude:** Practice gratitude by regularly acknowledging the positive aspects of your life. This can shift your focus from what is lacking to what is abundant, fostering a more optimistic outlook.

3. **Practice Mindfulness:** Mindfulness involves paying attention to the present moment without judgment. This can help you become more aware of your thoughts and emotions, enabling you to respond to them with greater clarity and intention.

4. **Build Strong Social Connections:** Nurture supportive relationships with friends, family, or mentors. Social support can provide a buffer against stress and offer valuable perspectives during challenging times.

5. **Seek Professional Help if Needed:** If you are struggling to cope with adversity, don't hesitate to seek professional help from a therapist or counselor. They can provide guidance and support in developing resilience skills.

Post-Traumatic Growth: Finding Strength in Difficult Times

While it may seem counterintuitive, adversity can sometimes lead to positive psychological changes, a phenomenon known as post-traumatic growth. This concept challenges the traditional view of trauma as solely damaging and suggests that individuals can not only recover from trauma but also experience personal growth and transformation.

Inspiring Stories of Post-Traumatic Growth:

Countless individuals have demonstrated remarkable resilience and found strength in the face of adversity. One such example is Malala Yousafzai, who, after being shot by the Taliban for advocating for girls' education, became a global icon for women's rights. Her story is a testament to the human spirit's ability to transcend trauma and emerge stronger than ever.

Factors that Contribute to Post-Traumatic Growth:

1. **Seeking Social Support:** Connecting with others who have experienced similar challenges can provide a sense of validation and belonging.

2. **Reframing the Narrative:** Reframing the traumatic experience as an opportunity for growth can empower individuals to find meaning and purpose in their suffering.

3. **Personal Reflection:** Engaging in personal reflection, such as journaling or therapy, can help individuals process their emotions and gain new insights into themselves and their experiences.

4. **Finding Meaning:** Discovering a sense of purpose or meaning after trauma can fuel resilience and inspire personal growth.

Understanding the psychology of resilience and embracing the possibility of post-traumatic growth allows us to navigate life's challenges with greater strength, wisdom, and hope.

Remember, adversity does not define us; our response to adversity shapes our character and determines our destiny. As Viktor Frankl, a Holocaust survivor and psychiatrist, famously said, "Between stimulus and response, there is a space. In that space is our power to choose our response. In our response lies our growth and our freedom."

Self-Reflection Questions:

1. **Personal Adversity:** Recall a challenging experience you faced in the past. How did you initially react to the adversity? What coping mechanisms did you use (both helpful and unhelpful)?

2. **Resilience Assessment:** On a scale of 1-10, how would you rate your current level of resilience? What specific aspects of resilience (adaptability, optimism, social support, etc.) do you feel strongest in, and which ones could be improved?

3. **Post-Traumatic Growth Potential:** Have you ever experienced a difficult event that led to positive changes in your life? If so, what were those changes? How did the experience shape your values, relationships, or outlook on life?

4. **Seeking Support:** When facing challenges, do you tend to isolate yourself or seek support from others? How could a stronger support system contribute to your resilience?

5. **Resilience Role Models:** Who are some individuals you know who demonstrate exceptional resilience? What qualities do they possess that you admire and would like to cultivate in yourself?

Transformative Exercises:

1. **Support Network Building:** Reach out to friends, family, or a therapist to strengthen your support network. Share your challenges and seek guidance from those who care about you.

2. **Post-Traumatic Growth Reflection:** If you've experienced a traumatic event, explore the concept of post-traumatic growth. Consider how the experience might have led to positive changes in your life, such as increased empathy, stronger relationships, or a greater appreciation for life.

3. **Resilience Skill-Building:** Identify specific resilience skills you'd like to develop (e.g., problem-solving, emotional regulation, stress management). Research techniques and strategies, and practice incorporating them into your daily life.

CHAPTER 7: HARNESSING THE POWER OF FOCUS - TAMING YOUR MONKEY MIND

"The mind is a wonderful servant but a terrible master." - Robin Sharma

Ever felt like your mind is a whirlwind of thoughts, constantly jumping from one idea to another? Like a mischievous monkey swinging through the branches of a tree, our minds often wander, making it difficult to focus on the task at hand. This phenomenon, usually called the "monkey mind," is a common experience in today's fast-paced world, where we are bombarded with information and stimuli from all directions. But what exactly is happening in our brains when we try to focus, and how can we tame our wandering minds?

Attention, the ability to concentrate on a specific object or task, is a complex cognitive process that involves several brain regions working together. The prefrontal cortex, located at the front of the brain, plays a crucial role in directing our attention and filtering out distractions. It acts as the control centre, coordinating the activity of other brain regions to ensure we stay focused on our goals.

However, the prefrontal cortex is not the only player in the attention game. The parietal lobe, situated at the top of the brain, helps us to orient our attention in space and time. It processes sensory information from our environment and helps us determine what to focus on and ignore. The thalamus, a relay station deep within the brain, also plays a role in attention by filtering incoming sensory information and directing it to the appropriate brain regions for further processing.

Despite the complex neural circuitry involved in attention, our ability to focus is often challenged by various factors. One major culprit is information overload. In today's digital age, we are constantly bombarded with a barrage of information from our phones, computers, televisions, and other devices. This constant stream of stimuli can overwhelm our brains, making it difficult to filter out distractions and focus on what is important. Similarly, multitasking, a common practice in our modern world, can also hinder our ability to focus. Research has shown that multitasking actually impairs our cognitive performance, wasting our time and mental energy, ultimately reducing our overall productivity.

Multitasking, another common practice in our modern world, can also hinder our ability to focus. While we may think we are more productive by juggling multiple tasks simultaneously, research has shown that multitasking actually impairs cognitive performance. When we switch our attention back and forth between tasks, we lose valuable time and mental energy, ultimately reducing our overall productivity.

So, how can we tame our monkey minds and harness the power of focus? The answer lies in understanding the science of attention and implementing strategies that promote focus and minimize distractions.

One effective technique is to create a conducive environment for focus. This may involve minimizing external distractions by turning off notifications, silencing our phones, and decluttering our workspaces. It also entails cultivating internal focus by practising mindfulness meditation, which can help to calm the mind and reduce mental chatter.

Another strategy is to prioritize our tasks and set clear goals. By identifying the most important tasks and allocating dedicated time to complete them, we can avoid feeling overwhelmed and maintain focus. Additionally, setting specific, measurable, achievable, relevant, and time-bound (SMART) goals can provide a clear sense of direction and motivation.

The Science of Attention: Understanding Focus and Distraction

Attention, the ability to focus our awareness on a specific object or task while filtering out distractions, is a fundamental cognitive function that underpins our ability to learn, work, and interact with the world around us. But what exactly is happening in our brains when we pay attention, and why do we sometimes find it so difficult to concentrate?

At its core, attention is a neural process that involves the coordinated activity of various brain regions. The prefrontal cortex, located at the front of the brain, plays a crucial role in directing our attention and filtering out distractions. It acts as the control center, coordinating the activity of other brain regions to ensure we stay focused on our goals.

However, the prefrontal cortex is not the only player in the attention game. The parietal lobe, situated at the top of the brain, helps us to orient our attention in space and time. It processes sensory information from our environment and helps us determine what to focus on and ignore. The thalamus, a relay station deep within the brain, also plays a role in attention by filtering incoming sensory information and directing it to the appropriate brain regions for further processing.

Attention is not a monolithic entity but rather a multifaceted phenomenon with different types. Selective attention refers to the ability to focus on a specific stimulus while ignoring others. Sustained attention, also known as vigilance, is the ability to maintain focus on a task over an extended period. Divided attention, however, involves attending to multiple stimuli or tasks simultaneously.

Our ability to maintain focus is not always perfect, and sometimes, we experience a phenomenon known as "attentional blink." This refers to the brief period of time when our attention is compromised after processing a stimulus. During this blink, we may miss other stimuli that occur in rapid succession, even if they are relevant to our goals.

The prefrontal cortex plays a crucial role in attentional control, the ability to direct our focus and resist distractions. This region of the brain is responsible for higher-order cognitive functions such as planning, decision-making, and impulse control. When we engage in tasks requiring sustained attention, the prefrontal cortex works to inhibit distracting stimuli and maintain our focus on the task.

Mindfulness Techniques: Training Your Brain to Be Present

In today's fast-paced world, our attention is constantly bombarded with a barrage of information and stimuli, making it increasingly difficult to maintain focus. However, mindfulness is a powerful tool that can help us tame our wandering minds and cultivate present-moment awareness.

Mindfulness is a practice that involves paying non-judgmental attention to our present-moment experiences, including our thoughts, feelings, and bodily sensations. It is about being fully present in the here and now, without getting caught up in the past or worrying about the future.

At the heart of mindfulness are several key principles:

- **Non-judgmental observation:** Observing our thoughts and emotions without labeling them as good or bad, right or wrong.
- **Acceptance:** Accepting our present-moment experiences as they are, without trying to change or resist them.
- **Letting go:** Letting go of thoughts and emotions without getting caught up in them.

Practising mindfulness regularly can train our brains to be more present and focused. This can lead to a variety of benefits, including reduced stress, improved focus, enhanced creativity, and greater emotional well-being.

There are many different mindfulness practices that you can incorporate into your daily routine. Some popular techniques include:

- **Guided meditations:** These involve listening to a recorded meditation that guides you through the process of focusing your attention and cultivating present-moment awareness.

- **Breathing exercises** involve focusing on your breath as it enters and leaves your body. By paying attention to the physical sensations of breathing, you can anchor yourself in the present moment and calm your mind.

- **Body scan:** This involves systematically focusing your attention on different parts of your body, noticing any sensations that arise without judgment.

Mindfulness is not a quick fix but a lifelong practice that requires patience and dedication. However, the scientific evidence suggests that it can be a powerful tool for improving focus, reducing stress, and enhancing overall well-being.

Self-Reflection Questions:

1. **Attentional Awareness:** How easily do you get distracted in your daily life? Are there specific activities or situations that consistently pull your focus away?

2. **Distraction Patterns:** What are your most common distractions? Are they external (e.g., notifications, interruptions) or internal (e.g., thoughts, worries)?

3. **Current Mindfulness:** How often do you find yourself fully present in the moment, without judgment or distraction? Are there moments when you naturally experience greater mindfulness?

4. **Mind Wandering:** How often does your mind wander during tasks or conversations? Do you find it easy to bring your focus back, or does it tend to drift away repeatedly?

5. **Attentional Impact:** How do distractions and mind wandering affect your productivity, relationships, and overall well-being? What are the potential benefits of cultivating greater focus and mindfulness?

Transformative Exercises:

1. **Mindful Observation:** Set a timer for five minutes and simply observe your surroundings without judgment. Notice the sights, sounds, smells, and sensations around you. When your mind wanders, gently guide it back to the present moment.

2. **Breathing Anchor:** Throughout the day, pause for a few moments and focus on your breath. Feel the rise and fall of your chest or abdomen, and let your breath serve as an anchor to the present moment.

3. **Body Scan Meditation:** Lie down or sit comfortably, and systematically bring your attention to each part of your body, starting with your toes and moving up to

your head. Notice any sensations without judgment, simply observing what is present.

4. **Distraction-Free Zone:** Designate a specific time and place in your day for focused work or relaxation. Eliminate distractions like notifications, clutter, and interruptions during this dedicated period.

5. **Mindful Task:** Choose a simple, routine activity like washing dishes or folding laundry. Engage in this task with full attention, noticing the sensations, movements, and details involved. This can help cultivate mindfulness in everyday moments.

CHAPTER 8: OPTIMIZING YOUR PHYSICAL HEALTH: THE MIND-BODY CONNECTION

"Take care of your body. It's the only place you have to live."
– Jim Rohn

This adage rings truer than ever as science unravels the intricate connection between our physical and mental health. It's no longer a question of whether our bodies and minds influence each other but rather a matter of understanding the depth and breadth of this profound relationship.

Consider this: A brisk walk in nature strengthens your muscles and cardiovascular system, but it also triggers a cascade of neurochemical reactions in your brain, releasing endorphins that elevate your mood and reduce stress. Similarly, a night of poor sleep doesn't just leave you feeling groggy; it can also impair your cognitive function, making it harder to focus, remember, and make decisions.

This mind-body connection is a two-way street. Just as our physical health can impact our mental well-being, our mental state can also affect our physical health. Chronic stress, for instance, has been linked to a wide range of physical ailments, including heart disease, high blood pressure, and weakened immune function. Conversely, positive emotions, such as joy and gratitude, have been shown to bolster our immune system and promote physical healing.

One of the most powerful tools for optimizing physical and mental health is exercise. Regular physical activity has been shown to profoundly impact our brains and bodies, offering a host of benefits that extend far beyond simply looking good.

Exercise is a natural stress reliever. When we engage in physical activity, our bodies release endorphins, which have mood-boosting and pain-relieving effects. These endorphins interact with receptors in the brain that reduce our perception of pain and trigger a positive feeling in the body, similar to that of morphine.

Exercise can reduce stress and improve mood. Studies have shown that regular physical activity can be as effective as medication in treating mild to moderate depression. This is because exercise increases the production of neurotransmitters like serotonin and dopamine, which are crucial in regulating our mood.

Moreover, exercise has been found to enhance cognitive function. Regular physical activity can improve our memory, attention, and processing speed. It can also protect our brains from age-related decline and reduce the risk of developing dementia and Alzheimer's disease. This is because exercise promotes the growth of new neurons and strengthens the connections between existing brain cells.

The benefits of exercise are not limited to the brain. Regular physical activity can also strengthen our bones and muscles, improve our cardiovascular health, reduce our risk of chronic diseases like diabetes and heart disease, and even help us to sleep better.

In light of these findings, exercise is not just a luxury but a necessity for optimal health. It is an investment in our physical and mental well-being, with returns that can last a lifetime. So, whether it's a brisk walk, a yoga class, or a weightlifting session, find a form of exercise you enjoy and make it a regular part of your life. Your body and mind will thank you.

The Role of Exercise in Mental Toughness

Exercise is not just about physical fitness; it's a powerful tool for cultivating mental toughness. Regular physical activity can fortify your mind, enhancing your ability to cope with stress, regulate your emotions, and boost your self-confidence.

Stress, a ubiquitous part of modern life, can wreak havoc on our mental well-being. However, exercise is a potent antidote to stress. When we exercise, our bodies release endorphins, natural mood elevators that can reduce feelings of anxiety and tension. Regular physical activity can also increase our tolerance for stress by improving our cardiovascular health and immune system.

Exercise also plays a crucial role in mood regulation. It can alleviate symptoms of depression and anxiety by increasing the production of neurotransmitters like serotonin and dopamine, which are essential for emotional balance. Additionally, exercise can provide a healthy outlet for pent-up emotions, helping us to process and constructively release negative feelings.

Self-confidence, a key component of mental toughness, can also be significantly boosted through exercise. When we achieve fitness goals or simply push ourselves to complete a challenging workout, we gain a sense of accomplishment and mastery that translates into greater self-belief. This increased self-confidence can then spill over into other areas of our lives, empowering us to tackle challenges with greater resilience and determination.

Different types of exercise offer unique benefits for mental health. Aerobic exercise, such as running, swimming, or cycling, is particularly effective in reducing stress and improving mood. Strength training can boost self-confidence and body image, while yoga and tai chi can promote relaxation and mindfulness. The key is to find activities that fit into your lifestyle that will make it more likely that you'll stick with them over the long term.

Incorporating exercise into your daily routine doesn't have to be complicated. Start with small, achievable goals, such as taking a brisk walk during your lunch break or doing a short yoga session before bed. Gradually increase the duration and intensity of your workouts as you become fitter. Remember, consistency is key. Even a small amount of exercise done regularly can significantly impact your mental health.

Nutrition for Cognitive Function: Fueling Your Brain

Just as our bodies need fuel to function properly, so do our brains. The food we eat plays a crucial role in our cognitive function, affecting our memory, concentration, and overall mental performance. A balanced diet rich in essential nutrients can optimize brain health, while a diet high in processed foods and sugar can impair cognitive function.

Omega-3 fatty acids, found in fatty fish like salmon and tuna, are essential for brain health. These healthy fats help to build and maintain cell membranes in the brain, promoting communication between neurons and enhancing cognitive function. Antioxidants, found in fruits and vegetables, protect the brain from damage caused by free radicals, which can contribute to cognitive decline. Vitamins, such as B vitamins and vitamin D, are also crucial for brain health, playing a role in energy production, neurotransmitter synthesis, and nerve function.

Processed foods, sugary drinks, and excessive caffeine can have a detrimental effect on cognitive function. These foods are often high in calories and low in nutrients, leading to blood sugar fluctuations that can impair brain function. Additionally, they can contribute to inflammation, which has been linked to cognitive decline and neurodegenerative diseases. Excessive caffeine can disrupt sleep patterns and lead to anxiety and jitters, further impairing cognitive function.

To optimize your brain health:

1. Focus on incorporating more whole, unprocessed foods into your diet.
2. Fill your plate with fruits, vegetables, whole grains, and lean protein.

3. Choose healthy fats, such as those found in olive oil, avocados, and nuts, over saturated and trans fats.

4. Limit your intake of processed foods, sugary drinks, and caffeine.

5. Stay hydrated by drinking plenty of water throughout the day.

Remember, food is not just fuel; it is medicine for your body and your brain. By nourishing your brain with a healthy diet, you can enhance your cognitive function, improve mental clarity, and protect your brain from age-related decline.

Self-Reflection Questions:

1. **Current Activity Level:** How physically active are you on a regular basis? Do you engage in exercise that you enjoy and that challenges you appropriately?

2. **Exercise and Mood:** Have you noticed any connection between your physical activity levels and your mood, energy levels, or overall mental well-being?

3. **Nutritional Habits:** How would you describe your typical eating patterns? Do you fuel your body with nutritious foods that support cognitive function and overall health?

4. **Mind-Body Awareness:** Are you attuned to the signals your body sends you about its needs for movement, rest, and nourishment? How can you improve this mind-body connection?

5. **Physical Health Goals:** What are your current goals for improving your physical health? How do these goals align with your broader aspirations for mental toughness and personal growth?

Transformative Exercises:

1. **Exercise Experiment:** Commit to trying a new form of exercise for a week. Choose something you've been curious about, whether it's dancing, hiking, swimming, or weightlifting. Observe how it affects your energy levels, mood, and overall well-being.

2. **Mindful Movement:** Incorporate mindful movement practices into your routine. This could involve yoga, tai chi, or simply walking in nature while focusing on your senses and the present moment. Notice how this affects your body and mind.

3. **Nutritional Upgrade:** Identify one area of your diet that could be improved. This could be increasing your intake of fruits and vegetables, reducing processed foods, or ensuring you're getting enough protein and healthy fats. Experiment with making this change for a week and observe the effects.

4. **Body Scan Meditation:** Practice a body scan meditation to enhance your mind-body connection. Lie down or sit comfortably, and systematically focus your attention on each part of your body, noticing any sensations without judgment.

CHAPTER 9: CREATING A SUPPORTIVE ENVIRONMENT - BUILDING YOUR TRIBE

"Alone we can do so little; together we can do so much." - Helen Keller

Humans are inherently social creatures, wired for connection and belonging. Throughout history, our survival and well-being have been deeply intertwined with our ability to form and maintain relationships. In the modern era, this fundamental need for social connection remains as vital as ever, especially when it comes to building mental toughness and resilience.

Research has consistently shown that social support plays a pivotal role in coping with stress, overcoming adversity, and achieving our goals. A strong network of supportive relationships can serve as a buffer against the challenges life throws our way, providing us with the emotional, practical, and informational resources we need to thrive.

When we face difficult times, having someone to lean on can make all the difference. Whether it's a friend who lends a listening ear, a family member who offers practical assistance, or a mentor who provides guidance and encouragement, social support can help us to feel less alone and more empowered to overcome obstacles.

Studies have shown that individuals with strong social support networks are less likely to experience depression, anxiety, and other mental health problems. They also tend to have better physical health outcomes, including lower blood pressure, stronger immune function, and faster recovery from illness.

The benefits of social support are not limited to times of crisis. Strong relationships can also enhance our daily lives by providing us with a sense of belonging, purpose, and meaning. They can offer opportunities for personal growth, learning, and self-discovery. Furthermore, social support can boost our self-esteem and confidence, making us feel valued and appreciated.

Social support acts as a catalyst for resilience in the context of building mental toughness. When we know we have people who believe in us and are willing to help us, we are more likely to persevere in the face of challenges and bounce back from setbacks with renewed vigor and determination.

Social support can take many forms. It can be emotional, such as listening, empathizing, and offering encouragement. It can be practical, such as providing financial assistance or helping with childcare. It can also be informational, such as offering advice or sharing knowledge.

The secret to a robust support network lies in its diversity. It should be able to cater to our various needs. This could include friends, family members, romantic partners, mentors, colleagues, or even online communities.

Building a strong support network takes time and effort. It involves being open and vulnerable, reaching out to others, and reciprocating support. It also means being a good listener, offering empathy, and being there for others when they need us.

The Importance of Social Support: Building Your Network

Humans are inherently social beings, wired for connection and belonging. Throughout history, our survival and well-being have been deeply intertwined with our ability to form and maintain social bonds. In today's world, where the pace of life is often frenetic and isolating, the importance of social support cannot be overstated.

Social support encompasses the various assistance and resources we receive from others. This support can manifest in different forms:

1. **Emotional Support** includes expressions of empathy, love, trust, and caring. It involves having someone listen to our concerns, validate our feelings, and offer comfort and encouragement.

2. **Informational Support:** This entails providing advice, suggestions, or guidance. It can be as simple as offering directions or as complex as helping someone navigate a difficult decision.

3. **Instrumental Support:** This involves tangible assistance, such as financial aid, practical help, or material resources. It can be a lifeline during times of crisis or simply a helping hand with everyday tasks.

4. **Appraisal Support** refers to feedback and affirmation that help us evaluate our abilities and self-worth. It can

boost our confidence and motivate us to pursue our goals.

The benefits of social support are far-reaching and profound. Studies have shown that strong social connections can reduce stress, boost mood, enhance our ability to cope with challenges, and even improve our physical health. People with strong social networks tend to have lower blood pressure, stronger immune systems, and a reduced risk of developing chronic diseases.

Conversely, social isolation and loneliness can have devastating consequences for our mental and physical well-being. Research has linked loneliness to an increased risk of depression, anxiety, cognitive decline, and even premature death.

Building a strong and diverse social network is an investment in our long-term health and happiness. Here are some practical tips:

1. **Join Clubs or Organizations:** Find groups that align with your interests and values. This can be a great way to meet like-minded people and build meaningful connections.

2. **Volunteer Your Time:** Helping others can be rewarding, as can connecting with your community and making a difference in the world.

3. **Reach Out to Friends and Family:** Nurture your existing relationships by staying in touch and making time for social activities.

4. **Attend Social Events:** Look for opportunities to meet new people, such as workshops, conferences, or social gatherings.

5. **Be Open and Approachable:** Smile, make eye contact, and strike up conversations with people you meet.

6. **Be a Good Listener:** Show genuine interest in others and their lives. This can help to build trust and deepen connections.

7. **Offer Support to Others:** Remember that social support is a two-way street. Be willing to offer help and support to others in your network.

Setting Healthy Boundaries: Protecting Your Mental Energy

In the pursuit of building mental toughness, it is crucial to recognize the importance of setting healthy boundaries. Boundaries are the limits we set to protect our physical, emotional, and mental well-being. They define what we are comfortable with and what we are not, helping us to maintain healthy relationships and avoid burnout.

There are different types of boundaries:

1. **Physical Boundaries:** These relate to our personal space and physical touch.

2. **Emotional Boundaries:** These pertain to our feelings and emotional well-being.

3. **Time Boundaries:** These involve how we manage our time and energy.

Setting and maintaining healthy boundaries can be challenging, especially if we are used to putting others' needs before our own. However, it is essential for our mental health and overall well-being. Here are some strategies:

1. **Learn to Say No:** It's okay to decline requests or invitations if they don't align with your priorities or values.

2. **Delegate Tasks:** Try to do only some things yourself. Delegate tasks to others whenever possible.

3. **Prioritize Self-Care:** Make time for activities that nourish your mind, body, and spirit. This could involve exercise, meditation, time in nature, or simply relaxing and recharging.

4. **Communicate Your Needs Clearly:** Let others know your boundaries and what you are comfortable with.

5. **Be Assertive:** Stand up for yourself and your needs. Don't be afraid to say no or speak up if someone crosses your boundaries.

6. **Be Consistent:** Enforce your boundaries consistently. This will help others to understand and respect your limits.

Setting healthy boundaries is not selfish; it is an act of self-love and self-preservation. By protecting our mental energy, we can build resilience, enhance our well-being, and thrive in all areas of our lives.

Self-Reflection Questions:

1. **Social Circle Assessment:** Who are the people you spend the most time with? How do they make you feel? Do they energize and uplift you, or do they drain your energy and leave you feeling depleted?

2. **Support System Evaluation:** Do you have people in your life who genuinely support your goals and aspirations? Are you able to turn to them for encouragement, guidance, and honest feedback?

3. **Boundary Awareness:** How comfortable are you setting boundaries with others? Are you able to say no to requests that don't align with your priorities, or do you often feel obligated to please others at your own expense?

4. **Energy Vampires:** Are there any people in your life who consistently leave you feeling drained or emotionally exhausted? How can you limit your exposure to these "energy vampires" while still maintaining healthy relationships?

5. **Ideal Tribe:** If you could design your ideal support network, what qualities would you look for in the people around you? How can you actively seek out and

cultivate relationships with individuals who embody these qualities?

Transformative Exercises:

1. **Support System Inventory:** Make a list of the people in your life who provide you with different types of support (emotional, practical, informational, etc.). Identify any gaps or areas where you could benefit from additional support.

2. **Boundary Setting Script:** Write a script for setting boundaries in various situations. Practice saying these scripts out loud until you feel more confident asserting your needs and priorities.

3. **Tribe Building Action Plan:** Create a plan for expanding your social circle and building your tribe. This could involve joining new groups, attending events, or reaching out to people you admire.

4. **Energy Audit:** Keep a journal for a week to track your energy levels before and after interacting with different people. Note any patterns or trends that emerge, and use this information to make informed decisions about how you spend your time and with whom.

5. **Gratitude Practice:** Cultivate gratitude for the supportive people in your life. Express your appreciation for their presence and contributions, whether through verbal affirmations, written notes, or acts of kindness.

CHAPTER 10: PUTTING IT ALL TOGETHER - YOUR PERSONAL MENTAL TOUGHNESS PLAN

"The difference between ordinary and extraordinary is that little extra." - Jimmy Johnson

As we embark on the final stage of this journey, it's time to take the knowledge and skills you've acquired and mold them into a personalized mental toughness plan. This plan will be your roadmap to achieving your goals, overcoming challenges, and living a more resilient and fulfilling life. It's about that "little extra" propelling you from ordinary to extraordinary.

The first step in creating you plan to conduct a thorough self-assessment. This involves taking an honest look at your strengths, weaknesses, and areas for growth in the realm of mental toughness. It's like taking inventory of your mental toolkit, identifying the tools you already have and those you need to acquire or sharpen.

Consider the following questions:

- What are your core values and beliefs?
- What motivates you?
- What are your strengths and weaknesses regarding self-discipline, focus, emotional regulation, resilience, and goal-setting?
- What challenges do you typically face in pursuing your goals?

- What strategies have you used in the past to overcome obstacles?

Reflecting on these questions will provide valuable insights into your current level of mental toughness and help you identify areas for improvement. You can also utilize various self-assessment tools, such as the Mental Toughness Questionnaire or the Grit Scale, to better understand your strengths and weaknesses.

Once you have a clear picture of your starting point, it's time to start crafting your personalized mental toughness plan. This plan should be tailored to your unique needs, goals, and circumstances. It should incorporate the strategies and techniques outlined in the previous chapters but focus on those that resonate most with you and address your specific challenges.

Your plan should include:

- **Clear, specific, and measurable goals:** What do you want to achieve? What steps will you take to get there? How will you measure your progress?

- **Actionable strategies:** What techniques will you use to enhance focus, manage emotions, build resilience, and cultivate self-discipline?

- **A timeline:** When will you implement these strategies? How will you track your progress and adjust your plan as needed?

- **Support system:** Who can you rely on for encouragement, guidance, and accountability?

Remember, your mental toughness plan is not set in stone. It's a dynamic document that should evolve as you grow and change. Be flexible and adaptable, and be bold and experiment with different strategies to find what works best for you.

Reflecting on Your Journey: Identifying Your Strengths and Weaknesses

Taking a moment to pause and reflect on your journey thus far is a crucial step in building mental toughness. By examining your personal experiences, challenges, and successes, you can gain valuable insights into your current level of resilience and identify areas where you would like to grow. This process of self-assessment is not about judgment or criticism; it's about honest self-reflection and a willingness to learn from your experiences.

To guide you in this process, consider the following questions and prompts:

- **Challenges:** What were some of the most difficult challenges you've faced in your life? How did you cope with them? What did you learn from those experiences?
- **Successes:** What are some of your proudest accomplishments? What strengths did you draw upon to achieve them? How did these successes contribute to your overall resilience?

- **Stressors:** What are the biggest sources of stress in your life right now? How do you typically respond to stress? Are there any patterns or tendencies that you notice?
- **Coping Mechanisms:** What strategies do you use to cope with stress, setbacks, and difficult emotions? Are these strategies healthy and effective?
- **Values:** What are your core values? How do they guide your decisions and actions?
- **Goals:** What are your personal and professional goals? How do they align with your values?
- **Self-Talk:** What kind of internal dialogue do you typically engage in? Is it positive and supportive, or negative and self-critical?
- **Support System:** Who are the people in your life who provide you with support and encouragement? How do they contribute to your resilience?

Take some time to journal about these questions, or discuss them with a trusted friend, family member, or mentor. As you reflect on your answers, be honest with yourself and avoid self-judgment. Remember, this is a journey of self-discovery, not self-criticism.

Interpreting Your Self-Assessment Results:

Once you've completed your self-assessment, take some time to analyze your responses. Look for patterns, recurring themes, and areas where you feel particularly strong or weak. What are your greatest strengths when it comes to mental toughness? What are the areas where you would like to improve?

Use your self-assessment results as a starting point for creating a personalized plan for ongoing growth. This plan should be tailored to your specific needs and goals, taking into account your strengths, weaknesses, and values.

Action Steps: Creating a Personalized Plan for Ongoing Growth

Building mental toughness is a continuous process that requires commitment, effort, and a willingness to embrace challenges. To create a personalized plan for ongoing growth, follow these action steps:

1. **Set SMART Goals:**

- **Specific:** Clearly define your goals. What exactly do you want to achieve?

- **Measurable:** Establish criteria for measuring your progress. How will you know if you are moving towards your goals?

- **Achievable:** Set goals that are challenging yet realistic. Don't set yourself up for failure by setting goals that are too difficult to reach.

- **Relevant:** Choose goals that align with your values and aspirations. Your goals should be meaningful and motivating to you.

- **Time-bound:** Set a deadline for achieving your goals. This will help you to stay focused and motivated.

2. **Break Down Large Goals into Smaller Steps:**

Don't be overwhelmed by the size of your goals. Break them down into smaller, more manageable steps. This will make them seem less daunting and more achievable.

3. **Identify Potential Obstacles:**

What are some of the challenges that you might face as you work towards your goals? Be proactive and identify potential obstacles so that you can develop strategies for overcoming them.

4. **Develop Strategies for Overcoming Obstacles:**

For each obstacle, brainstorm several possible solutions. Think about what has worked for you in the past, and consider seeking advice from others who have faced similar challenges.

5. **Track Your Progress:**

Regularly track your progress towards your goals. This will help you to stay motivated and see how far you've come. Celebrate your successes, no matter how small they may seem.

6. **Adjust Your Plan as Needed:**

Life is unpredictable, and your goals may change over time. Be flexible and willing to adjust your plan as needed. If you encounter unexpected obstacles or setbacks, don't give up. Learn from your experiences and adapt your approach.

Remember, building mental toughness is a journey, not a destination. Embrace the challenges, learn from your mistakes, and never stop growing. As you cultivate resilience and inner strength, you will discover a newfound sense of empowerment and a greater capacity to thrive in the face of adversity.

CONCLUSION: EMBRACING A LIFETIME OF MENTAL TOUGHNESS - YOUR JOURNEY CONTINUES

"Life's not about how hard of a hit you can give... It's about how many you can take and still keep moving forward." – Sylvester Stallone

As we conclude this exploration of mental toughness, let us reflect upon the key takeaways and empowering strategies unfolding throughout our journey.

We began by delving into the essence of mental toughness, recognizing its significance in navigating life's challenges and achieving our goals. We examined the power of self-belief and how cultivating an "I can" attitude can propel us forward despite adversity. We learned to identify our values and align our actions with them, fostering a sense of purpose and direction that strengthens our resolve.

In exploring habits, we uncovered the science behind habit formation and learned how to break free from detrimental patterns while establishing positive ones. We discovered the importance of self-discipline and the role it plays in staying committed to our goals, even when faced with temptations and distractions.

Understanding our emotions became a focal point as we explored the intricate interplay between our thoughts, feelings, and actions. We gained insights into the significance of emotional intelligence and developed strategies for managing our emotions effectively, turning them into allies rather than adversaries.

The power of focus took center stage as we examined the science of attention and learned techniques to tame our wandering minds. We embraced mindfulness to cultivate present-moment awareness, enabling us to channel our mental energy effectively.

Recognizing the profound connection between our physical and mental well-being, we delved into optimizing our physical health. We discovered the transformative effects of exercise on our mood, cognitive function, and overall resilience.

Reflecting on these key takeaways, we must remember that building mental toughness is not a one-time event but an ongoing journey. It requires continuous effort, self-reflection, and a willingness to learn and grow. Embrace the challenges and setbacks as opportunities for growth, and never lose sight of your goals.

"The man who moves a mountain begins by carrying away small stones." - Confucius

Remember, you possess an inherent strength and capacity for resilience. You have the power to overcome obstacles, achieve your dreams, and live a life of purpose and fulfilment. Embrace the journey of building mental toughness and unlock your full potential. The path may be challenging, but the rewards are immeasurable.

In the words of Winston Churchill, "Success is not final, failure is not fatal: it is the courage to continue that counts." So, go forth with courage, determination, and an unyielding spirit. Embrace the challenges, learn from your experiences, and never stop growing. Your mental toughness is your most valuable asset; nurture, cultivate, and watch as it transforms your life.

Dear Reader,

Thank you for embarking on this journey of building mental toughness with me. I am deeply grateful that you invested your time and energy in exploring the strategies and insights within these pages. I hope that you find valuable tools to help you navigate life's challenges, cultivate resilience, and ultimately achieve your goals.

If you found this book helpful and inspiring, **I would be honoured if you would consider leaving a review on Amazon and rating "Building Mental Toughness."** Your feedback is invaluable to me as an author, and it helps others discover the potential within these pages.

Once again, I want to thank you for your readership. Your commitment to building mental toughness is inspiring. I am here to support you on your path, and I wish you continued strength, growth, and success in reaching your goals.

With sincere gratitude,

Brianna Brooks

www.ingramcontent.com/pod-product-compliance
Lightning Source LLC
Chambersburg PA
CBHW071216240526
45470CB00018B/1873